Marina Flores is a poet, writer, and all around a queer kid. A marketing professional, Marina hones in on the best demographic she knows (herself), and while growing up in a small immigrant community, she expresses herself the only way she can, through writing. Marina developed her skills in poetry over the years, connecting and supporting the LGBTQIAP+, Chicanx, Immigrant, and POC communities. She and her twin sister were among the first in their family to pursue higher education, and both earned a Bachelors in Communication and a Minor in English. Marina's first publication came at the age of 25 and three more soon followed, all for poetry. Marina currently lives in the Los Angeles area with her partner, their dog, Roxy, and her extensive hat collection.

Dedicated to Mrs. Lamb, for believing in me.

Marina Flores

A JOURNAL ENTRY

I hope you enjoy
the read!

Marina Flores

AUSTIN MACAULEY PUBLISHERS™

LONDON · CAMBRIDGE · NEW YORK · SHARJAH

Ordering Information
Quantity sales: Special discounts are available on quantity purchases by corporations, associations, and others. For details, contact the publisher at the address below.

Publisher's Cataloging-in-Publication data
Flores, Marina
A Journal Entry

ISBN 9781685620264 (Paperback)
ISBN 9781685620271 (ePub e-book)

Library of Congress Control Number: 2022915560

www.austinmacauley.com/us

First Published 2022
Austin Macauley Publishers LLC
40 Wall Street, 33rd Floor, Suite 3302
New York, NY 10005
USA

mail-usa@austinmacauley.com
+1 (646) 5125767

I would like to give thanks to my siblings: Alfonso, Tony, and Marisa Flores, and to my mother, Alma Cordero, for the constant encouragement and inspiration. To my friends: Mary Jane Carignan, Kara Dempsey, Alejandro Bañuelos, Maya Tayrien, Ashley Moore, Esther Kim, and many other friends and family for proof reading, know-how, criticism, and of course, inspiration. Thank you to my partner, Sidney White, for being my muse, and diligently telling me to keep trying. Thank you to my professors and teachers for sharpening my skills. Above all else, thanks be to God.

Table of Contents

To Thine Own Self Be True

It's like walking against the tide
The whole world pushes against you
They tell you what must be

But to thine own self be true

I cannot lie
I cannot lie to myself

To thine own self be true

I walk against the tide

I'm going to hold her hand
I'm going to kiss her
I'm going to love her

I will walk against the tide
Even if the whole world pushes back

A Hole in My Chest

A hole in my chest
I feel like lead
I am a human statue come to life

I am so cold
Empty hands
My feet are heavy

I keep my chin up
As my eyes well with tears
A smile to my face
A hole in my chest

Don't Look

Don't look, she says
Don't look

But how can I?

I crave her
I long
I lust
I love

Don't look

I weave through a maze
How will she find me
If I don't look

On Screen

It comes naturally
Like I knew it would

The tears in my eyes
The ache in my heart

Why does it hurt so much
Why does it sting

I'm wringing my hands
But I can't look away

It happens every time I watch these lesbian music videos
But I can't look away

A piece of me on screen

Not My World

When I'm out in public
And I see a pretty girl
I often don't know what to say
What to do

And I am reminded
Every single time
Of my position

I am not safe
This is not my world

But still
I often look
I smile
I pretend not to be afraid

Kaleidoscope

I feel like I'm in a kaleidoscope
I don't know which way is up
I don't know which way is down
There is color all around
And all I seem to do is frown

I look this way and that
I am out of place
I can feel something is wrong
And I fear by the time I figure it out
I'll already be long gone

A Love like Mine

I'm scouring the internet
And I can find almost nothing that looks like me
A boy and a girl together
All these narratives of love
Not one of a girl and a girl

How I search and long for a story that resembles mine
Not one of two women holding hands
One stealing a kiss
The other blushing

How they would hold each other in the middle of the night

I can find nothing of the love I know so well

Legs and Skin

I have dreams at night
And sometimes during the day
They're usually about a girl
They're always about a girl

And she's in my arms
I'm wrapped up in her
A pretzel knot of legs and skin

How

I'm sewing my chest back together
My hands are oddly steady as the blood drips from them
Why do I picture myself in a crooked form
My heart beats so steady in the palm of my hand
It falls with a terrible thud

How do you pick it up so easily
That angelic smile on your face
Putting the pieces of my heart back together

Do Not Put Me on a Pedestal

Do not put me on a pedestal
I am not to be admired
I am not to be looked at
I am not a thing

Do not put me in a glass case
I am not made of gold

I am a human being
Speak to me
And I will answer
Play music
And I will dance

I am made of flesh and blood
I am to think
To breathe
To live

Do not put me on a pedestal

Dysphoria

The words that ring in your ear
What exactly do you hear
You're pulling out your hair
Your hands are on your face
You wish you were wearing lace

Self-harm does have its charm
Your words are so provocative
You better put a lock on it
Boys are from Venus
Girls are from Mars
Tell me who's in charge

The Spell

It's the way she speaks
English, but mixed in a way I've never heard before
As if all the letters and words put together were completely
new

She enchants me
A spell every time she speaks
I hang on every word

Scholar

To learn from you
To learn of you

A scholar
What I would do to sift through your pages

Neurons

I could lie with her
And think of nothing
While all the neurons in my brain are firing

Magnet

It is never enough, I am a magnet
Pulled to you by some invisible force

Close

I need to touch you
Skin on skin

Her Heart

I can feel my heart shudder
It bounces in place
My throat is closed
My hands are clasped

The way she looks at me
She makes my heart race
I turn toward her
And she holds my gaze

As she comes near
I begin to stand
She puts her hand in mine
And I can feel her heart, beat to beat

You Look Like a Girl Today

"You look like a girl today"
Every time I wear a dress
Never fails
I am a woman already
Why isn't that enough

"You look like a girl today"
What did you think I was before
As if a dress proves who I am
A silly garment

I wish I could tear off my skin and show you what's inside
Am I woman enough for you now

Age

She moves slowly because of the pain
I help her undress
My mother's back is thin
Her muscles are weak

I put on her socks for her
Dressed again, I am forced to watch her squirm into a comfortable position
I cannot touch
I cannot carry
I'll hurt her
So I watch the struggle

At last
Laid down to rest
I tuck my mother in
Roles reversed
So this is age

Princess

The damsel in distress
Princess
Goldilocks
You keep putting us in a box

Only good looking until you say we are
Who you fight dragons for

Did you ever stop to think that maybe you are the dragon
Only set free because you have the key
But you're the one who made the cage
Can't you see why we're in such a rage

It's despicable
How you admire our feathers and put us in a cage
Rejoice when you open the door that you yourself shut

Are you blind or stupid

He Can No Longer Hurt You

He can no longer hurt you
She said
And I could feel myself rise
She repeated
He can no longer hurt you
I felt myself rise still
Like a hot air balloon filled with fire

It is today
Today I hurl the bags over the cliff
Today
I release my anger
Today
I let the burden go
It is today
That I am free

There is no anger left in me
I am set free
Hallelujah

Boom

I'm ready to date
But what they're really saying is
I'm ready to fall in love

Because that's really what's happening
But people are afraid
Afraid of love
Of vulnerability
They push them away
Self-sabotage
Destruction
Boom

Confetti

Look at you
Happy in your pseudo vulnerability
Content in your proximity

You are an Easter egg
Fun to play with
Bright and colorful
But hollow inside

Confetti
Fluff
Sparkles
You lack substance

What was it again
You don't like labels
I'm sure you don't

The Only Constant Is Change

The only constant is change
Everything is changing

It's important to find small pieces of peace
The trees so green
I still find the butterflies dance together
And that the dragonflies like to play

The summer breeze has always seemed to soothe me

Cactus

Red flowers and purple flowers
And I
Standing here
A cactus
Can no one see past my thorns

Seasons

The ground is sodden
And the sun seems to rise from the trees
The air is awash with freshness
And I am standing with glee

The green has suddenly appeared on the mountains
And the rivers are flowing free
The land is constantly changing
And the same goes for me

In the Fields They Grow

Butterflies are drifting on by like petals in the wind

The poppies in the fields
Orange blossoms like freckles on a child's face

Hayley Kiyoko

It radiates with me
Pulls on a thread I didn't know was there

My eyes begin to water
My heart throbs in my chest

The words that chase me
I'm the only one in a game called it

The soothing ache
I'm not alone

"Girls like girls, like boys do, nothing new"

Heart Race

Make my heart race
You dubious creature
The thing that dances
The thing that sings

Make my heart race
Make my tongue dance
Keep me enthralled
Keep me excited

Let's make the lover's dance
Take the chance
It's tonight
It's today
Take me away—Take my hand

Resigned

There are never enough hours in the day
Yet they drag on
I can never get enough done
There is always more

The hours stretch
And I am resigned
How long the hours fold

I am sitting in my desk chair
Staring out into the sun

Unraveled Dolls

Schizo—something or other
Not schizophrenia
Something else
A different diagnosis
They have different categories
That's what she called it

And it amazes me
How much people can suffer
How they can still go on

She told me something else too
It gives you compassion
To know what people go through
To diagnose

To unravel the thread
See them bare
What great impact
Direct result
The unraveled dolls
To see the beauty underneath

Times Are Strange

Times are strange
Stress and anxiety
Piled up on each other like blocks
Watch how the child, called life, stacks them
Now watch them tumble and fall

Nothing is ever constant
No matter how tall

Bare Skin

I don't recognize the woman in the mirror
With colored lips and eye lashes
A painted face
I feel like a clown

"You look pretty today"
Wasn't I already
Those lips that leave
Stains on my skin

I want my face bare
Look at me
This is who I am

Ravenous

We all have a hunger
And I am ravenous
To fill the empty void in my chest

It's not about finding someone
It's about BEING SOMEONE

So let me sing, damn it
Let me dance
Let me love out loud

I want to hold her
To kiss her
To make love in the middle of the fucking night
With screams of joy

It's not who I love
But that I love
And I have so much love to give
I am RAVENOUS
To love as I love is no crime or sin, but the manifestation of
such joy that angels sing

So I will love out loud

I will be myself

And no matter the persecution, execution, I will not fall into retribution

I am myself

And I am most myself when she is with me

Chemistry

Electric
The currents of me
Passing through the currents of her

A reverberation
The molecules of my skin connecting to hers

We are a molecular structure
Our very atoms bond
It's more than chemistry

The Shadow Men

I see men made out of shadow
They don't come at night
But day

The shadow men
Who mean no harm
Who watch
Who do not speak

The shadow men
I see at the corner of my eye
The shadow men
Who won't say goodbye

Ghosts

Every acquisition of a premonition, I must go into submission because with every ghost I see, I feel like I'm losing me

And I know I may or may not be schizophrenic, but please listen to my rhetoric
With every metaphor and simile, there is no soliloquy
I'm trying to tell you a story

Now listen
I see ghosts day and night
Some whisper
Others hide
They look like shadows
Always at the corner of my eye

I don't know why God gave me this evolution. Are they trying to find some retribution? I'm lost in confusion. What is this contusion? I need answers. Did they die from cancer? Is this fate? What do I do if I'm in the monster's wake? I will not be bait

These demons and ghouls, prostitutes and fools. I am no angel. Find some other angle. This is not my fable

Dripping Heart

I don't know how to convey intimacy
I want to say I love you
But the words don't seem heavy enough
They don't grasp all that I carry

My heart is dripping like a wet rag
Would you let my heart ooze between your fingers

For my love is messy
I am clumsy
And I don't know what I'm doing

But I'll give it to you
My heart

My dripping heart
My dripping heart that's so heavy it falls from my chest

Dream of Her

She and I
I'm attached to her like glue
My hand on some place of her

She's smiling at me
And I can't help but to smile back
I pull her close
Face to face

Then I get an email on my screen
None of it was real
It's never real
None of it
I can only dream

In the middle of the day
At night
On my drive home from work
I dream of her
And it's never real
But I dream of her

Slurs

It was a language rooted in hatred
A vile language
All in glistening white
Look at them sparkle
The words that tear my skin

Here for You

I know you have demons
I have them too
I know they can't go away
They're stuck with you

But I wish
With all my heart
To make them
Fall apart

PTSD is in no way a kindness
I wish I could cast some sort of blindness
You don't have to go through this alone
I know the cut hurts you down to the bone

I wish I could show you
What kind of beast you are
The courage you have
Will take you far

You have demons
I have them too
They won't go away
But I'm here with you

Death

What is death but a subtle creature

To spring upon us in the everlasting light
Never with a shock or a boom
To reach us in that knowing gloom

Death is as it ever was

Neither enemy nor friend
Calling us to find our end

Point

I think of it like pointillism

Each point is a speck that
When come together with other specks
Becomes a picture or a painting

So imagine us a speck, a dot, a point

Each one of us a different color

We are points
Part of a picture

We are the points on the portrait of
The face of God

Love Language

I know that it hurts you
It hurts you when you can't say I love you out loud
When the words get stuck to the roof of your mouth
When you can't say I love you in my language

But, darling
Don't you understand
I've learned yours

I know you love me
You've said it a hundred times
In a thousand different ways

And I love you too

Robin's Egg

Unable to think
Or perhaps thinking too much
My head is swimming with thoughts

The way you look at me
Like no one has before

I have never been cherished

You hold me like a robin's egg in your hand

Brave Again

I can tell you when I'm afraid
When I don't feel brave anymore
When I feel like a child again
And I'm afraid of what goes bump in the night

It's you who soothes me
Who reminds me of who I am

The blacksmith to my knight in shining armor
You make me brave again

In Perfect Agony

I'm lying in perfect agony
I scream silently
I've become quite good at crying quietly

It's another night
And I'm drowning in my tears
A cliché, I know
But this time it's true
Because I can't catch my breath
My eyes are water fountains and my chest heaves
Still not a sound
I have nothing to hold onto as I claw in the dark
My blankets are a tangled mess
Water flows through my face like a river bed
And I lie there alone in perfect agony

To Steal a Kiss

To steal a kiss

I'm in a romance novel
A global pandemic
And I can think of nothing but you

I've sent letters and videos and poems and prose
Anything to reach out to you
And it's never enough

What my hands could say what my words cannot

To steal a kiss

Sunshine

I can feel the silence creeping
It will stay here for days on end
An unwelcomed guest

One that takes up too much space
I can feel it in every room
I don't know how to shut it out

This emptiness is massive
Like fog
It fills your lungs

Only you
My sunshine
Could make the day warm again

This House Is Empty

This house is empty and quiet
It longs to hear your voice
The pitter patter of your foot steps
The music in the way you move

Only each other for company
Silence
Nothing for either of us to say

The house looks at me
And I it
We both miss you

No Color

I feel a great loss in my heart without you
I feel empty
How many different ways can I say I miss you

Ten
Ten million

It doesn't matter
It all means the same

The world has no color without you

Jessie's Girl

I don't know why it hurt so badly
That woman's voice
I heard her sing on the radio
A familiar song
Jessie's girl
And everything changed
Because suddenly I was the woman singing
I felt it
The words that sting
Like a slap
Harsh
Sudden

And I was a young girl again
Confused
Unsure of my feelings
And yet
Wanting more of what I didn't understand

"I wish I had Jessie's girl," she sang
I understood
Because I wanted her too

Photo

I understand why photos in wallets are always tattered and
torn
I find myself scrolling, scrolling in my phone to find the one
picture I have of you

I could stare at it for hours
Trying to remember every inch of your face
Wondering when I'll see you again

Everything

I want everything
I want every single piece
I don't want a piece of the pie
I want the whole damn cake

I want the ugly
I want every single thread
I want the beauty
Give me the droplets of dew on silk, I'll eat them up
Give me every passion and emotion and single thought
running through your head
I want to hear it all

I want the cruel
The pain, the animosity, the fumbling and flabbergasting,
everlasting procrastinating
I want it all

Give me the tear drops and empty thoughts
Every inclination and divine inspiration
Give me your art, give me your failures, give me every
fallen knee

I'll take them all

I want every breath
I want every sigh
I want every moment of darkness
I want the light
I want the shadows and the whispers
I want the cries at night

Give me the roaring laughter
Give me the unbearable tears and all of your fears
I'll carry them
I want everything
I want to be able to count the stars in your chest
Let me make a constellation of your heart
I'll find the galaxy of your mind
And I'll let you trace the stars on my spine

I want everything
I want the solar system of you
And I'll give you my universe

Brood Like a Flame

Old friendships brood like a flame
Soft
Like a candle light

Months could pass
And it'd be the same
As if I saw you yesterday

Years pass
And I still look for your flame in the dark

Praise the Lord

Praise the Lord
For without you I am nothing
In the midst of my wake
It is you who comforts me

My Pen and I

My pen and I know each other well
Harbor your gifts, I was told
Cultivate them
Watch them grow

My pen and I
We work together side by side
Practice makes perfect
"One more"
She says to me

Trees

The trees are so tall
I watch them reach for the heavens
These creatures of God
Who ask for nothing

These great beasts
Who are so gentle
They fill the air in my lungs

I Am a Monster

Mirror, mirror, on the wall
Who's the beast I see after all

Creature, creature is it me
Is that who I see

Is there something wrong
For how long

There is so much distortion
What a horrible fortune

Panic rising in my chest
Farewell to those that knew me best

There is no imposter
I am a monster

Trapped in My Own Head

Trapped in my own head
Is this what it feels like
To go insane

Unable to trust myself
Subconscious
Conscious
My mind is playing tricks on me
I don't trust what I see
Let me be free

I can hear the bars clacking
My mind is attacking

Blanket

Nightmares that pull me close
Like a blanket over my face
Suffocating

So hot
But you can't release your blanket
It's your shield
Against the things that go bump in the night

Abduction

Interception
Detention
My mind is a cave
I am a slave

Upon this ship
I cannot equip
I am guinea pig
About to lose my lid

I have been sent
To become an experiment
They do as they please
With so much ease
I am on my knees

Woe Is Me Woe Is Me

Woe is me woe is me
The world is dark
And I am stark

Friends are away
I cannot go out and play
So much to delay

Fret not, says the little whisper in my ear
How queer
I stay inside
And abide abide
To that little whisper in my ear

I Move Forward

The world is slow
And I
In constant direction
Projection
I look back

Slowly, it turns
Too fast to keep up
I move forward

You Are My Summer

It's cold
But you keep me warm

Such comfort
To bury my face in the crook of your neck

It's winter finally
But you are my summer here

What a Beautiful Day

There is something in the delight of sitting outside
My meal is fresh
My drink is just right
And my macaron is waiting for me

I like to look at the clouds as I eat
What a beautiful canvas
What a beautiful day

Misery

Misery
My old enemy
You still think you can conquer me

To Jabberwock and vorpal sword
We go to battle of my own accord

To night and day
I will keep these monsters at bay

The beast within
Will be chagrin
For the succession of depression shall not be the only
aggression
The tribulation of alienation is a retaliation of such mental
stimulation
These comrades in arm
Only wish to do me harm

Misery
A deity
But what is it to me

A heathen
I bring my own legion

Bring me a war
And I will settle the score

At hells' gate
I create my own fate

Lose to you
I'd never do

A samurai
I'd rather die

Horror

Why do I believe in God
I have seen too many spirits
Too many ghosts and devils
I cannot deny God
But I can only hope for heaven

I do not seek horror
I dwell in it
I live it
I am it

Frozen

There are things I want to say
And there are things I can't say
They come wrapped up in the same box
The words hanging on the edge of my lip
Repeated over and over again in my head
The way she looks at me
The words frozen on my tongue

A Knife's Blade

There is a curl of hair when I put my hair up
It reminds me of a knife's blade
I look into my own eyes
And I pierce my skin

My own skin
That lock of hair
Reminds me of a knife's blade

Held up to my neck
A knife's blade
I pierce my own skin

Be Strong

I'm sorry
You will feel it through me

Prepare for the stares
The murmuring
Gestures and slurs

They're going to follow me around the store
I will be pulled over with no violation
People will cross the street
They'll speak to me in a language I don't know

And you will feel all of this through me
My love
I'm so sorry
This is my world
Be strong

Beauty Underneath

What a strange, wonderful feeling
I've never experienced it before

To be appreciated
Not the long stare that you've known since you were twelve
years old by the men across the street

No
This is different
This seeing all of me
And seeing the beauty underneath

Everyone Has Gone Away

It's lonely here
It's so quiet
Everyone has gone away

It's dark
The world is grey

Only the birds to soothe me
But they never stay

I speak to the trees
But they never have a word to say

Fear Licks My Chin

I can feel it
I am falling in cascades
Shattering

There is no room for anxiety attacks
There is only emptiness
I am hollow

I can feel my heart beat in my chest
But is it there
I keep kicking dust where I once stood

Fear licks my chin

How Dare You

How dare you
Stagger back into my life without so much as a knock on
the door

What delusion is this
To think that you loved me
Fool

With all your gas lighting and fighting
Criticize and minimize everything I had ever done

What's worse
You acknowledge this
Yet no apology
No retribution to the attribution you gave to my contusion

What right have you to speak to me
None
None at all

How Do You Enchant Me

How do you enchant me
That even your scent is alluring to me

That when I kiss you
You have to remind me to breathe